曾美霞著

文史哲詩叢

山 動 了

文史哲出版社印行

Encountered numerous coincidences
In life
The sage
Knows very well
　How to handle
　　The beauty of
　　　Every moment

人生是
無數的偶然

智者
善於把握
每一個
美

的
片
刻

序

——美麗而婉約的心情

能用最簡潔生動的文字，來表達情感和事物；能假藉單純的形象塑造一個優美的境界，讓自己或讀者的心靈均能陶醉浸染其中，就是好詩。

曾美霞女士是位全能的作家，其從事教育工作二十餘年，業餘從事寫作，她的散文和小說早已膾炙人口；寫詩時間雖然不算很長，但其作品別見風格，婉約柔美。

她能兼顧老師、母親、妻子的工作，尚能寫出不少作品，固然是她的先生——小說家陳韶華兄的薰陶；但也由於她溫婉誠摯的個性，常在其作品中自然流露出一種特有的風格，一種美麗而婉約的心情，隱約含蓄於作品之中。

在「生命的存摺」中，她寫：

生命是一本存摺

綠蒂

載著一次次成長的喜悅

載著一次次提領的驚心

感傷存摺上的結餘

又被揮霍掉

一些歲月

以及「山動了」、「石與水」等首均深含人生哲理。「旅程中的母子」、「紅磚道」等溫馨感人，「底片」、「咖啡屋」等情懷浪漫、抒情幽美。

以一個「業餘」的女詩人能有這樣的作品，十分難得。寄望她能更深入詩的領域，以更豐盈詩的作品，來充實生命的旅程，這是我的祝福。

在我赴以色列出席第十三屆世界詩人大會前夕，她的詩集要出版了，臨上機前，寫上我祝語；願她這份美麗而婉約的心情，在詩中，以及在現實的生活中，永遠持有。

目錄

山動了

功名的韁索繫控了你
痳痺了你的眞摯誠樸
你的心　不動如山

利祿的鐐銬套牢了你
麻木了你的善良純潔
你的情　不動如山

現實的網絡　絲絲紊紊
交織繞纏　束縛了你
癱瘓了你的仁慈溫柔
你的心你的情

冬眠成繭　不動如山

山啊　來一次沸騰的爆發

繭啊　來一次掙裂的蛻變

讓燒熔的情　激越

讓震撼的心　悸顫

讓　不動的

山　動了

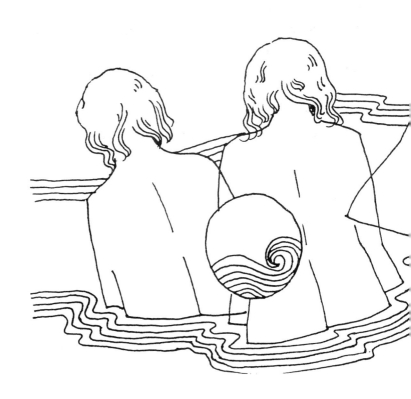

THE MOUNTAIN IS MOVING

Tied up by a rope of achievements and accomplishments
Your sincerity and honest were paralyzed
And your heart, unmovable, as a mountain

Shackled and handcuffed by wealth and high positions
Your gentleness and pureness were benumbed
And your emotion, unmovable, as a mountain

The net of practicalism
Caught you as trapped by cobwebs
Your kindness and tenderness were gone
Your heart, your emotion
Hibernated as a cocoon, unmovable, as a mountain

Oh, mountain, stage an explosion
Oh, silkorm in the cocoon, make a break-through
Let the melting emotion, burn
Let the trembling heart, shake
Let the unmovable
Mountain, move

BETWEEN TWO POINTS

In that year
I had many beautiful dreams in my world
And you were emancipated and free in your kingdom
You told me: between two points
The most shortest distance is a stright line
You walked to me and knocked my dreams
I said: I love the winding streams
Much more than a straight and even waterway
Since then, you brought me
To watch sunrise in mountains
To listen sea-waves along the beach
To hear birds singing in the woods
To pick stars in outskirts
To appreciate the lotus in a park
And to take a walk around the curving path
After made numerous turns
Finally arrived
In your kingdom
Appeared in my dreamland today
Only you

兩點之間

那年
我在我的天地做著美夢
你在你的王國揮灑自如
你說　兩點之間
最短的距離是直線
你大步走來敲我的夢
我說　我愛蜿蜒溪流
勝過平直溝渠
於是　你帶著我
攀登山峰　觀日
繞行海邊　聽濤
彎入林中　聞鳥

都是你
我的每個夢
到了你的王國
如今
轉過多少曲折
繞了多少彎路
折回公園　賞荷
轉往郊野　摘星

仁愛路的楓

秋　漸黃了仁愛路
走在行道樹下
浴著濃郁的楓香
晃耀的雜黃和碎綠
擾得方寸空懸
如果一樹殷紅是奢望
至少讓我期待艷麗的橙
不速的過客老虎
逼退了沁冷的寒意
燒熔了造物者的朱彩
蒸乾了我的玫瑰紅酒
失望的楓啊

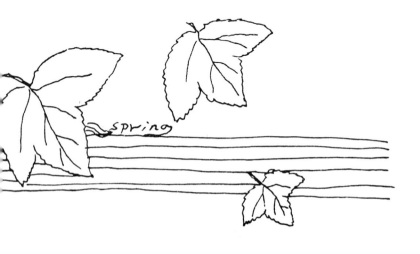

來不及披上紅衫
片片萎落磚道
沮喪的我啊
無從醉紅兩腮
踽踽獨行仁愛路上
啊　蒼白的我
就拾一兜　枯黃的楓
題上幾首詩吧

太平山的枯木

超卓的鶴立
矮樹林中那一桿高直
娓娓訴與白雲
那曾經擁有的聳然

耀眼的雪亮
綠樹叢裡那一身皙白
喃喃吟向藍天
那曾經煥發的燦然

任嚴寒冬臨
滿山萎黃咒詛凍凝的嵐

等來年春暖
一樹青綠頌歌新吐的芽
那孤傲依舊不馴
那挺立依舊突兀

風風　雨雨
絮絮　叨叨
太平山的枯木啊
把千年的盟約
銘記在心底
將永恆的誓言
鐫刻在枯白的軀幹上
日日　月月
歲歲　年年

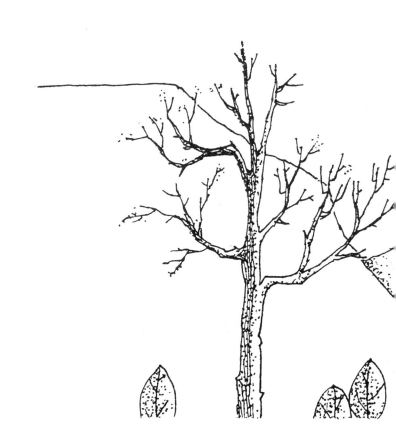

生命的存摺

生命是一本存摺

載著一次次成長的喜悅

愛吃蛋糕的年紀

我喜歡點燃蠟燭

唱著　數著

炫耀存摺上的戳記

又努力累積了

一些歲月

生命是一本存摺

載著一次次提領的驚心

怕吃蛋糕的年紀

我不敢吹熄蠟燭
忍見燭蕊飄升的
縷縷輕烟
感傷存摺上的結餘
又被揮霍掉
一些歲月

LIFE'S SAVINGS ACCOUNT

Life is a book of savings account
Recording the happiness of growth
At the age of fondness for eatin cakes
I'm glad to light candles
Singing and counting
The amount of my account is increasing
By hardships
Through a number of months and years

Life is a book of savings account
Recording the frightener of withdrawals
At the age of fear for eating cakes
I was scared to blow out candles
And watched the smoke
Raising and dispelling
The balance of my life's savings account
Were squandered
Through a number of months and years

RIVER OF TIME

If the memory
Flows like water
Then, the time passes like a river

Time passed as a shallow creek
Drifting murmuringly
And the memories in it were so clear and pure

The time slipped out of my fingers
Carried things of the past
Falling into the gurgling river
Amid the running current
Were soft voices and light smile

In front of my eyes roars the river as years gone by
Things of the past pick up from it
Are so muddy and filthy
Make me frightened and hoodwinked
Oh, how can I look back

歲月的河

歲月就是河流

記憶是水

如果

掬起的記憶明澄純淨

流失的時光清淺

曾是涓涓小溪

指間滑落的時光

帶著往事點點滴滴

落入琤琤琮琮的溪流

迤邐著細語輕笑

小溪潺湲壯大奔騰
眼前是洶湧江河
奔逝的歲月浩瀚
盛起的往事紛杳渾濁
心驚　豈僅驀然
慨嘆　怎堪回首

石與水

《之一》石

臥在河床上的石
像參差而固執的男人
突兀聳立的石
任流水迴旋腳底
儼然中流砥柱
輕巧圓潤的石
逐波而流沈浮不定
只能隨遇而安
小石身不由己
戀戀仰視
那卓絕堅毅的俊拔

《之二》水

那恬淡無爭的適意
欣羨俯瞰
大石孤高傲寂

當她靜止端肅
她是冷冷的鏡

當她起伏流轉
她是不可捉摸的光陰

淙淙慢流　令人消沉無奈
湍急激盪　使人心神不寧

山中觀瀑
海岸聽濤
溪邊掬水
一種水　百樣千貌

百樣千貌的水

是百樣千貌的女人
水的別名
是女人

《之三》　石與水

柔弱的水緩緩流經
堅硬的石
輕撫粗糙的臉
低語中
夾雜細碎嬌笑
偶有極微的啜泣
屹立的石　不爲所動

春去春來
歲歲年年
柔弱的水　柔弱依然
那英姿勃煥的石啊

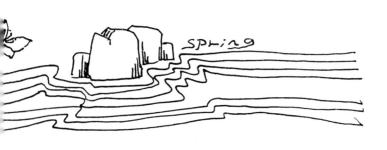

那孤傲堅毅的石啊
削瘦了雄壯
磨平了粗獷
嶙峋崢嶸呵
豪邁頑桀呵
不復再見
柔弱的水緩緩流經
曾是堅硬的石

秋風

陽春的風暖煦
花草怯怯招展　迎風
仲夏的風涼適
遊子汲汲破浪　乘風
深秋的風啊　蕭颯含羞

含羞草的閉合是心靈的
顫抖
秋愁的沉澱是思念的
結晶
暖春溶化在奔放的長夏
長夏失落在悸動的深秋

深秋是一廂情願的無奈

好個秋

好個孤獨瑟縮的秋

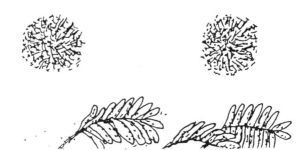

AUTUMNAL WIND

The warm wind in early spring
Made flowers and grasses waving in the breeze
The cool wind in hot summer
Made travellers ride on waves restlessly against the wind
And the autumnal wind was chilly and shy

The opening and closing of mimosa leaves
Were the trembling heart and soul
The sediment of autumnal sorrow
Was a crystallized remembrance
The warm spring melted in a bold, long hot summer
And the long hot summer got lost in a palpitated autumn

The autumn was deeply attached to helplessness
What a autumn
A solitary, dreary autumn

CIRCLES

A single legged compasses
Couldn't draw a circle
So, it searched and waited, finally
Found another leg
They swore to draw the circle in same central point
And drew the circle in different radiuses
They drew together a concurrent circle
Perhaps not perfect
At least could cover each other
If they don't want to adjust the radius
They could insist their own principle
But if they have no way to keep their oath
They should move the central point away
Otherwise, the three interlocked circles
Would cut each other
And cause the three circles
In separation and breakage

圓

想畫個圓
單腳的圓規
尋覓　等待　終於
找到另一半
以不同的誓言爲圓心
以不同的原則爲半徑
畫的是同心圓
也許不完美
至少能包容
如果不想調整半徑
可以堅持各自的原則
如果無法固守誓言

就該把圓心移到遠方
因爲三個交錯的圓
只會互相切割
使每個圓
支離　破碎

葉脈

從樹梢飄落
如繽紛落英　願化泥護樹
秋風不解　拂過清流淨石
依舊是高掛枝頭的黛綠
猶帶著花開時節的芳香
無奈却飄墜污泥

求甘霖　雨水更泛漲了污泥
盼春暉　陽光却蒸腐了身軀
暴虐蹂躪了敏銳自尊
豐腴消蝕蕩然
只剩得澀白的嶙峋枯骨

拈一葉淒美藏扉頁

讓冷傲伴黛玉

長住紅樓尋夢

忘却仲夏綠荷舊憶

春風多事　無端亂翻書

吹掀傷心情懷

勾起前塵往事

唏噓　唏噓

LEAF VEINS

The autumnal wind blew over clear water and clean rock
Caused numerous petals and leaves
Fell down to the ground to cover the roots
It couldn't understand why leaves fell down to the mud
Were still green
And carrying blooming fragrant

Leaves begged for a shower, but a storm flooded the mud
Leaves yearned for light of spring, but the sun decayed its body
Your selfrespect was devastated in cruelty
Your plumpness was fading away
Only craggy bones were leftovers

I picked up a piece of sadness and beauty and hid in a book
Let it stayed in the Red Chamber
With Miss Lin Tai-yu
And forgot those memories under green lamps
However, the spring wind unintentionally opened the book
Discovered the hiding sadness
And things of the past
Drew a long sigh

DIGITALIS

It gives flowers
In a line, shaped as bells
Looks like wind bells
Swing silently in wind
When the wind is rising
They shake soundlessly
Oh
Those muted wind bells

It gives flowers
High up in mountains, shaped as bells
Looks like gentlemen
Waving softly in wind
When the wind is rising
They assume airs of importance
Oh
Those disguised hypocrites

Oh, digitalis
If your emotional involvements are continual
You don't have to be selfderived
Perhaps your smile in wind
Is imitating prostitutes
Pretending to attract customers

Oh, digitalis
You have already cut off your worldly affairs
You don't need to exhibit your colorful attires
Perhaps your selfexile in mountains
Is learning from politicians
Pretending to secure high positions

毛地黃

朵朵鐘形小花
排列有序成行
彷彿串串風鈴

風來
靜默地隨風搖晃
悄然無聲

哦
瘖啞的風鈴

朵朵鐘形小花
開在高高山上
儼然飄逸雅士

風來
柔媚地迎風招展
搖首弄姿

哦
作態的雅士

啊　毛地黃
若果塵緣未了
又何須自棄麗質
莫非風中的嬌笑
只是學那流鶯
欲迎還拒

啊　毛地黃
既已遠離塵囂
又何須姹紫嫣紅

莫非山中的解放
只是學那政客
以退爲進

spring

山中傳奇

那片林
翁翁鬱鬱芬菲莽莽
修竹青翠

那午后
雲蒸霞蔚秋雨新霽
鳥鳴清脆

那使君
乍然驚艷信誓旦旦
願爲卿瘁

FOLKTALE IN MOUNTAINS

那羅敷
翩翩回眸朱唇微啓
嫣然輕啐

In that forest
Long and green bamboos
Were grown widely, thickly and richly scented

In that afternoon
Birds were singing in roseate clouds
After an autumnal shower

That young man
Suddenly fell in love with a lady and took oath
Willing to die for her

And that married lady
Gracefully glanced back and slightly opened her lips
Spat merrily upon him

泛黃話匣子

掀開被記憶塵封的話匣子
銹了發條的音樂不成調
一逕伊唔

泛黃的相片
是署名影中人的小黃帽
敍述的童話

泛黃的信紙
是簽著知名不具的船型帽
訴說的神話

泛黃的日記
是自稱only you的大方帽
傾吐的情話

至於那
泛黃的喜柬
是兩姓共同具名的雙方
傳佈的
所謂的
佳話

泛黃的淚珠滴落
銹了發條的伊唔
變成一逕的吶喊
謊話　　謊話
謊話

旅程中的母子

那列火車　猛然啓動前行
那對母子　陡的驚懼後仰
兒子說　只是慣性定理使然
母親說　爲了抗拒時光匆促

欲捕攝窗外景物
兒子説
過去的難以捉摸
未來的不可測
唯有把握眼前的一幕
眼前的一幕却總是
在彈指間　飛逝

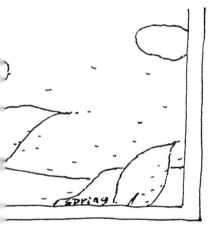
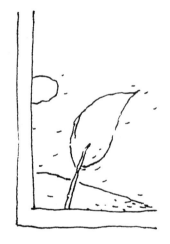

想細述窗外景物

母親說

熟悉的畫面是走過的軌跡

不斷重現的雷同

是千篇一律的人生

追求的是不平凡

刻骨銘心　却在另一段旅程

女王與神女

她粧扮起來
迎向一群群興奮的人們
從日出到日落
張開雙臂　接受歡呼
賓客來時　她微笑
眞誠　或無意識
已然厭倦却　不容厭倦
日落卸粧　她解衣
把小心珍藏的
向唯一的他　展露

spring

她粧扮起來
迎向一張張興奮的面孔
從黃昏到清晨
張開雙臂　接受歡呼
賓客來時　她解衣
真誠　或無意識
已然厭倦却　不容厭倦
清晨卸粧　她微笑
把小心珍藏的
向唯一的他　展露

生之喜悅

掙脫溫暖的莢

趁著那陣抖動

孤獨地墜落塵埃

　　無怨　無尤

　　無悔　無言

泥濘的浸漬　軟了硬殼

烈日的酷曬　裂了包膜

　　當風雨襲來

伸出細弱的根

緊緊抓住大地

　　當甘露降臨

適時張開稚嫩的口　吸吮

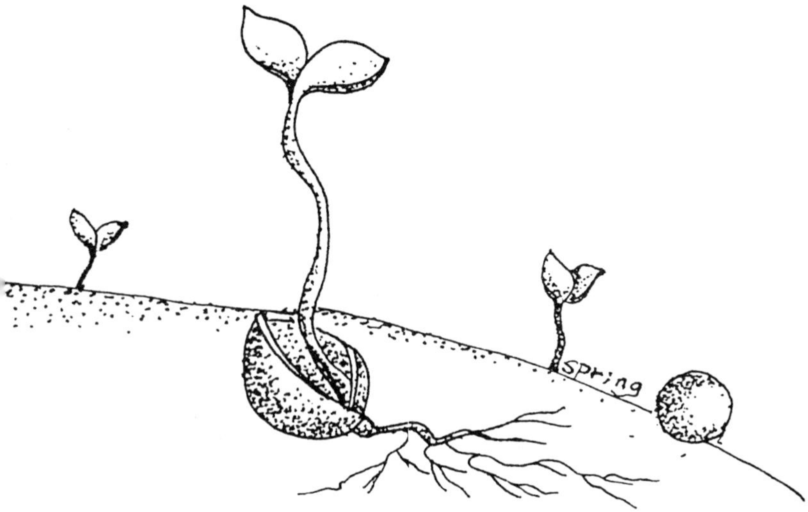

HAPPINESS OF BIRTH

啊　終於萌出幼芽
生命的喜悅
原是來自痛苦

Untrammelled from a warm pods
Shaking off boundness
You fell to the ground in solitude
Without hatred, without complaint
No regret, in silence
Your hard shell was softened in mud
Your membrane was broken in hot sun
When storm came
You stretched out your tiny roots
And grapped the great earth with all strength
When it was raining
You opened your immatured mouths to absorb and suck in time
Oh, finally, young sprouts
Brought happiness of life
Actually, it arrived with great pains

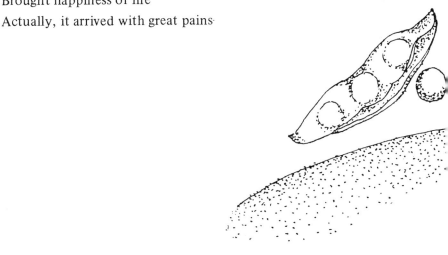

紅磚道

踏過一羣羣年輕的制服

灑落串串笑語

踩過一對對依偎的情侶

浮現滿地浪漫

跑過一隊隊童稚的小腳

漾出一片天真

不經意的

夜幕籠罩了大地

一列列暗紅的地氈

被黑夜染得更深紫

再沒有溫馨　再沒有喧鬧

只有孤獨的旅人

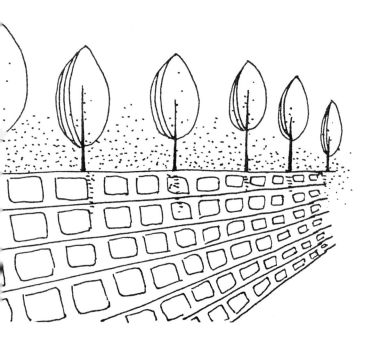

迤邐著疲憊的身軀
在空洞的寒夜裏
諦聽著冷寂的跫音

底片

我求妳
為我的憂鬱診脈
妳笑飛了滿天處方
我捕捉一篋嬌笑
攝入思念的心版

想找一些快樂的理由
取出珍藏的底片
暗房加重了我的憂鬱

青碧的山水　腥紅
烏黑的長髮　灰白

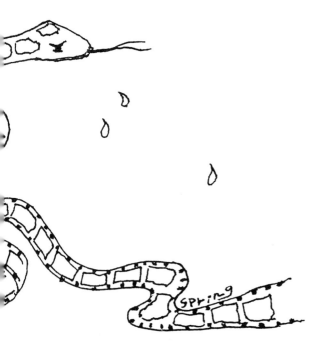

嫣紅的櫻唇　慘綠
潔白的貝齒　濁污

啊　魂夢爲勞的妳呀
待我把一切翻轉
不知妳的笑
是否依然

NEGATIVES

I asked you
To examine my pulse of melancholy
You laughed and made diagnosises flew in the air
I caught a piece of smile
Printed on my longing heart

Wished to find out reasons of happiness
I took out my treasured negatives
The dark-room caused my melancholy mood more heavier

The greenish mountain and river have turned into blood-red
The blacky hair has turned into gray and white
The redish lips have turned into dull green
And the snow-white teeth have turned into dirtiness

Oh, your soul, exhausted by dreams
Should I overturn all of it
I couldn't tell
Whether the smile is still on your face

FALL DOWN

If you have experienced a falling down
Then, you know that kind of feeling
A real falling down
Came suddenly, not by your willingness
Precautionary measures were useless, no way to avoid it

There are many ways to walk into a river
I know how to walk into a river
I understand how to jump into a river
However, I'm not clear
How to fall into the river of love
I have no experience and don't know the way
You can sneer at me
But don't scold me
You can hate me with envy
But don't insult me

I'm now falling into the river of love
Unawarely and innocently

跌

如果你跌過
就懂得那感覺
真正的跌
突如其來　非你所願
預警無效　防備不了

進入河的方式很多
走入一條河　我瞭解
跳入一條河　我清楚
只有一種叫人不明白
跌入愛河　我茫然無措
我茫然無所措

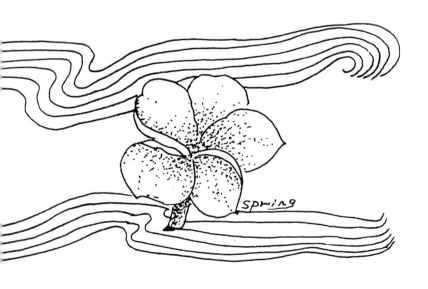

你可以嘲笑
但不能責怪
你可以妒羨
但請別辱罵

跌入愛河　我懵懂無辜
我懵懂又無辜

倒立

妳總是說我窮
妳總是說我醜
親愛的相信我
世界會改變
只要跟我一起來倒立
雙手撐起地球
星星就在腳下
瓜田儘管納履
李下何妨整冠
說什麼頂天立地
我能把天地調換
說什麼春去秋來

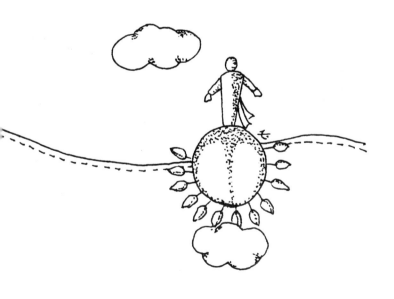

我能把時序扭轉

妳的秀髮既無法披肩

他的長袖又怎能善舞

富翁的口袋將不再麥克

窮人的阮囊又何必羞澀

親愛的不要走

請妳說說爲什麼

妳的拒絕還沒有變點頭

即使在反常的那片刻

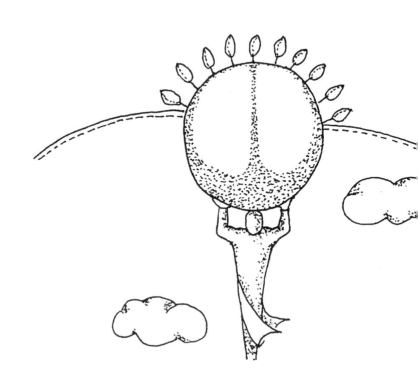

向天空

向天空張眼
我只能凝望
凝望白雲在天
凝望是凝望
天是天
雲是雲
我是我
你呢
你在何方
向天空閉眼
我才能遙想

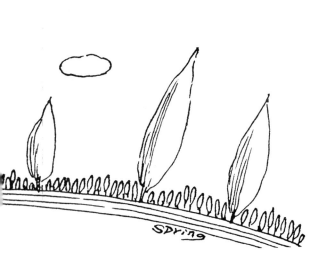

遙想白雲在天

遙想再遙想

天是你

雲是我

我是你的翅

你呢

你在我心中

TOWARDS THE SKY

Open my eyes towards the sky
I can only look
Look at the white cloud in the sky
Look is look
Sky is sky
Cloud is cloud
I'm still I am
And you
Where are you

Close my eyes towards the sky
I can only think
Thinking over the white cloud in the sky
Thinking after thinking
Sky is you
Cloud is me
I'm your wing
And you
You are in my heart

甲子端陽

節約用水的廣告言猶在耳
鬧鐘響起却一腳踩在水裏
屋裏屋外　汪洋一片
灰黑土黃　混濁一團
文明的街道泥黑
荒野的小徑腐臭
綴著霓虹燈的屋簷下
泡著那掙脫皮革的脚
跟水打仗
是都市人夏季大事
嘴裏咒著
不是缺水就淹水

spring

只有未來的主人翁

才有興趣欣賞

老天爺送的應節大禮物

到處都能划龍船

好一場即時大雨

咖啡屋

屋外　亮麗的陽光灑落一地
屋裏　孃孃的烟霧瀰漫一室
濃郁的香氣在冷氣流中瑟縮
只一會功夫
騰騰熱氣化爲冷漠
棕櫚樹旁　纏綿的熱戀情侶
置週遭陰冷於度外
臨街窗口　寂寞的長髮女郎
無視於窗外的擾攘
陰晦幽暗凝不住戀人熾燃的情
吸一口　相視微笑
好香的咖啡

喧囂熱鬧暖不了落單淒冷的心

啜一口　搖頭嘆息

好苦的咖啡

無題

走了
你用狐疑在臉上畫出問號
走了
我用感嘆給你一個肯定
一千多頁日曆　換來數不清
黏黏稠稠的記憶
你說別離難　難捨舊情
我說相見難　難逢舊友
你堅持不讓步
我決定不妥協
爲的是
讓爭執凍凝別離的憂傷

你知道我瀟灑的背包裡

裝滿無奈

我明白你爽朗的嘴角

掛著苦笑

於是我們說

相見時難別亦難

最難更是

從這次離別後

到下次相見前

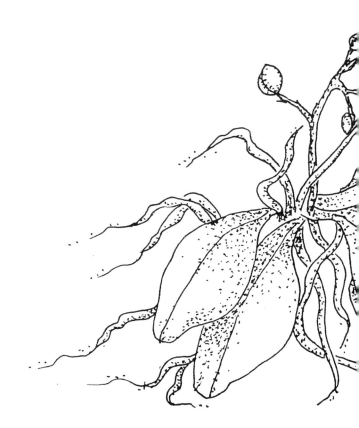

詩文之戀

你說
文是飯　詩是酒
又說
無飯令人瘦　無酒令人俗
於是
你用熱情舉炊　粒粒渴慕
我用相思釀酒　滴滴呼喚

踏著皎潔月色　攜一簞食
披著燦爛星光　提一壺酒
啜飲我的詩　吟來聲聲寂寥
咀嚼你的文　讀出朵朵烈焰

月落時

酒足飯飽　欣然凝望

星沉後

兩心契合　渾然忘我

懷念

是月光的嗚咽
抑是河水的低泣
今夜的夢境
爲何如此憂傷
盈滿於耳際的
儘是一片淒切

我迎向月光
想攬住一些亮潔
月光却無奈地搖著頭
逸入雲層

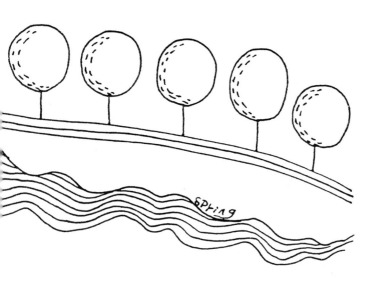

我奔向河水
想掬起一些清澄
河水却冷漠地揮著手
離我遠去

河水啊河水
莫非因著人們的貪婪

難道由於人們的無知
清純的人性被金錢污染
高貴的良知被金錢踐踏
任憑月光吶喊
任憑河水呼喚
終抵不過金錢的誘惑

月光啊月光
爲何不再照拂
爲何不再淙淙

於是月光晦暗
於是河水乾枯
於是可愛的故鄉晦暗乾枯

懷念

　　懷念

　　　　懷念

懷念月光籠罩
河水潺潺的故鄉
只有在夢中追尋
而今夜的夢境
却是如此的憂傷

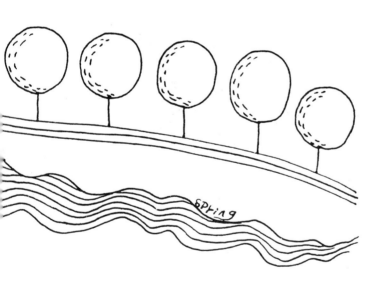

REMEMBRANCE

Why my dreams
Were so sorrowful tonight
The disconsolated noise
Overflowing in my ears
Were sobs of the moon
Or weeps of the river

I went to the moonshine
Tried to hold the clearness
But the moon shaked her head
And hid in clouds

I ran to the river
Tried to seize the cleanness
But the river waved her hands
And walked away

Oh, moon
Why you shone us no more
Perhaps the people were greedy
Oh, river
Why you flowed no more
Only for the people were ignorant
Their nature have been contaminated by money
Their conscience have been ruined by gold
No matter what moon shouted
No matter what river called
They couldn't resist the temptation of wealth

The moon is getting dark
The river is getting dry
And my lovely homeland is also getting dark and dry
Remember
　　　　Remember
　　　　　　Remember
I remember the moon shone in old days
And the river flowed in my homeland at that time
Those remembrances only can be searched in dreamland
But in my dreams tonight
Are so sorrowful

畢業

日西沉　月東升

熊熊的營火漸漸弱了

熱情的歡聚即將結束

幾本日曆　厚厚的一疊日子

你在這裏長大　成熟

多年以前

你展露好奇的笑容走來

轉眼　無數的時光飛逝

你將帶著我的祝福離去

今夜　此時

你我仍然歡笑在一起

明日　此刻

勞燕已然各自分飛去

明知留不住

　　却是捨不得

縱然忘不了

　　偏要強顏揮手

是太高興　抑或太傷心

爲何你我的雙眼

　　盈滿酸甜的汁液

畢業總是可喜

請你欣悅地離開

別離畢竟傷感

請你眞誠地謹記

去吧　　去吧

雖然淚眼婆娑

我終於看到你潛然的微笑

　啊　雨中綻放的百合

去吧 去吧

　　別猶疑 莫徬徨

勇敢地向前邁進

只是 別忘了

千萬別忘了

我將深深祝福你

——不僅在此時

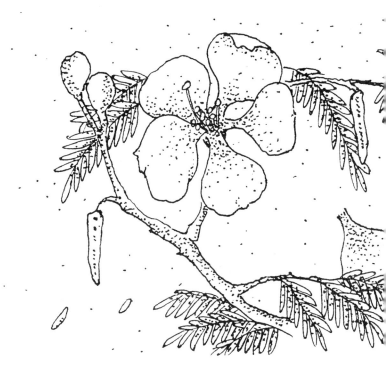

返鄉人潮

那裏是
人口密度最高的地方
有喧嘩擾攘
焦急浮躁的氛圍
那裏是
花錢耗時費神的地方
有汗臭擁塞
污濁閉滯的氣息
說過多少次
再也不去
却還是
無奈地走向它

只因爲
故鄉在呼喚
只因爲
母親在期盼
我又再做一次沙丁魚
浮游在人海裏
只爲了
趕回家鄉
只爲了
惦念親娘

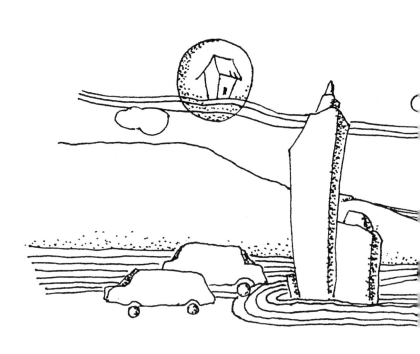

夕陽

月亮的離去
最是輕描淡寫
徐徐　徐徐
逸入漸明的光炫中

星星說再見時
喜歡眨一眨眼
眨落滿眶晶瑩的露珠
在荷葉上滾動　風乾

夕陽的告別
總是大事渲染

長睫只是隱約霧濕
揉搓紅腫的眼
揮撒一輪依依嬌嗔
只爲塗抹滿天憐楚
隨興潑灑彤雲
掃翻調色盤
任意甩動水袖
夕陽的告別
總是大事渲染
總是在黃昏
揪勒千百年來的人們
獻出多愁的心
一次次無悔的擲向
夕陽謝幕的舞台

刀販

小販嘶聲的吼

他有最利的剪　無論你多堅靱

他有最快的刀　任憑你多頑固

他有最尖的錐　不管你多強硬

他有最銳的鋸　哪怕你多結實

小販啞了　却自豪著

他販售了勝利的征服

在熱鬧的市集　對喧囂的人群

小販嘶聲的吼

他有最熱的情　無論妳多冷漠

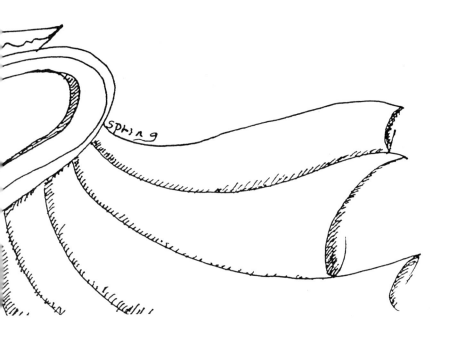

他有最深的愛　任憑妳多絕情

他有最柔的心　不管妳多寡義

他有最善的意　哪怕妳多狡點

小販啞了　更自卑著

他出賣了男性的尊嚴

在陰冷的窠巢　對霜寒的艷容

小販嘶聲的吼

剪不開　切不入

刺不進　割不斷

小販啞了

看不透　捨不得

在滿室的尖銳中奔竄

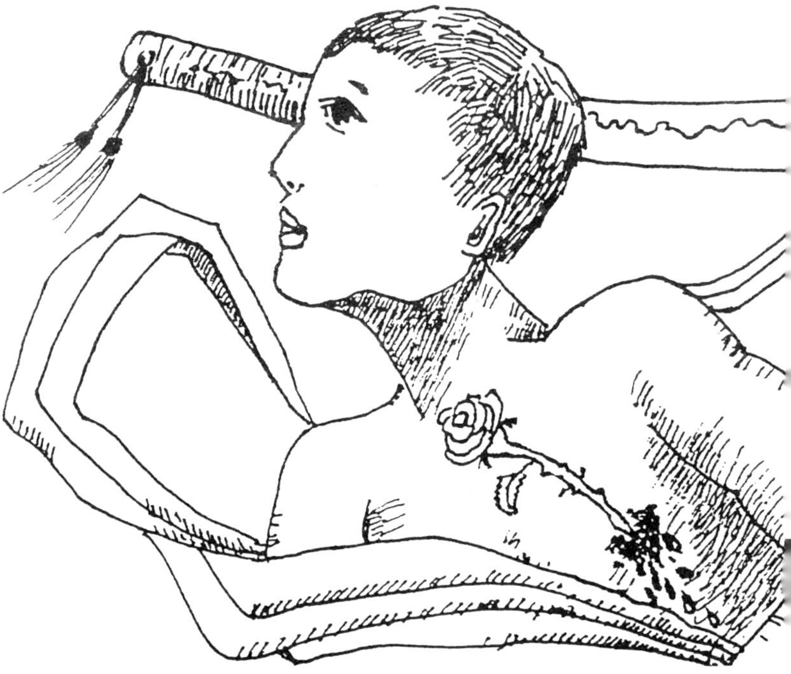

盈屋的銳尖淌血

小販的心淌血

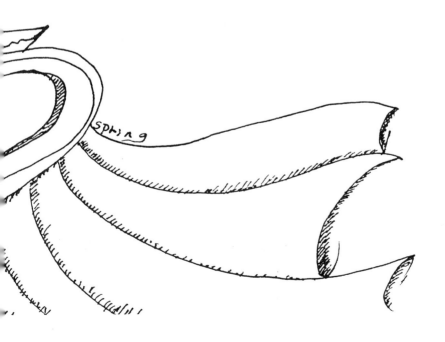

spring

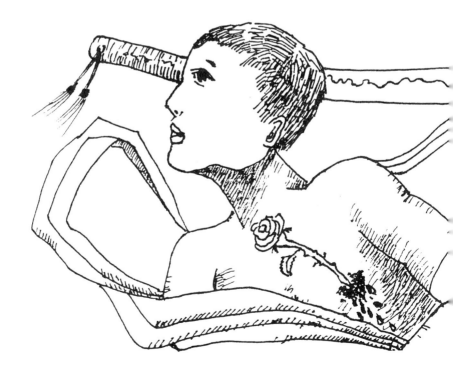

愛神的翅

曾經　相知相憐

何時　竟成陌路

我心不渝　他已遠颺

低語仍在耳際縈繞

眼裡滿是我　心裡滿是我

而今冷言如酷霜

緣盡情已了　何必再相見

啊　愛神

我殷殷的盼　切切的等

奈何

祢姍姍的來　又匆匆的走

任我聲聲呼喚　淚眼血紅

善變的動物
因祢羞見兩足的
只是想要急急飛離凡塵
不是爲了儘快降臨人間
祢那美麗雙翅‧……
邱比特　我終於知曉
總喚不回　尋不著

WINGS OF CUPID

We were intimated friends
And now become strangers
I haven't changed, but he walked away
His soft voice is still in my ears
In his eyes, he sees nothing but me
In his mind, he thinks nothing only me
And now, he treated me so cool
Our emotional involvements were terminated
Why should we meet again
Oh, Cupid, I'm waiting patiently, wishing sincerely
However, in hopelessness
You arrived late and left quick
I cried and my tearing eyes turned redish
Couldn't call you back
I have known at last, Cupid
Your beautiful wings brought you not to the earth
But flew you away from us
Because you were ashamed to see
The unfaithful animal walking with two legs

秋憶

悄悄的　楓葉就紅了
正如無聲的　鼻酸
遠遠的　西風瑟縮著
就像抽搐的情感
憶著過往的日子
踩著未來的歲月
燦亮的嫣笑之下
隱透著幾許感傷
多少的人　深印腦海
多少的事，迴盪心底
多少的物　重現眸際
抖落一季憂鬱

却揮不去深濃的懷念
想你　想你
——在深秋

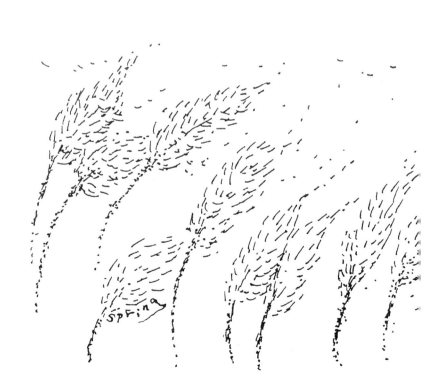

懷思

——敬悼陳徐瑟女士

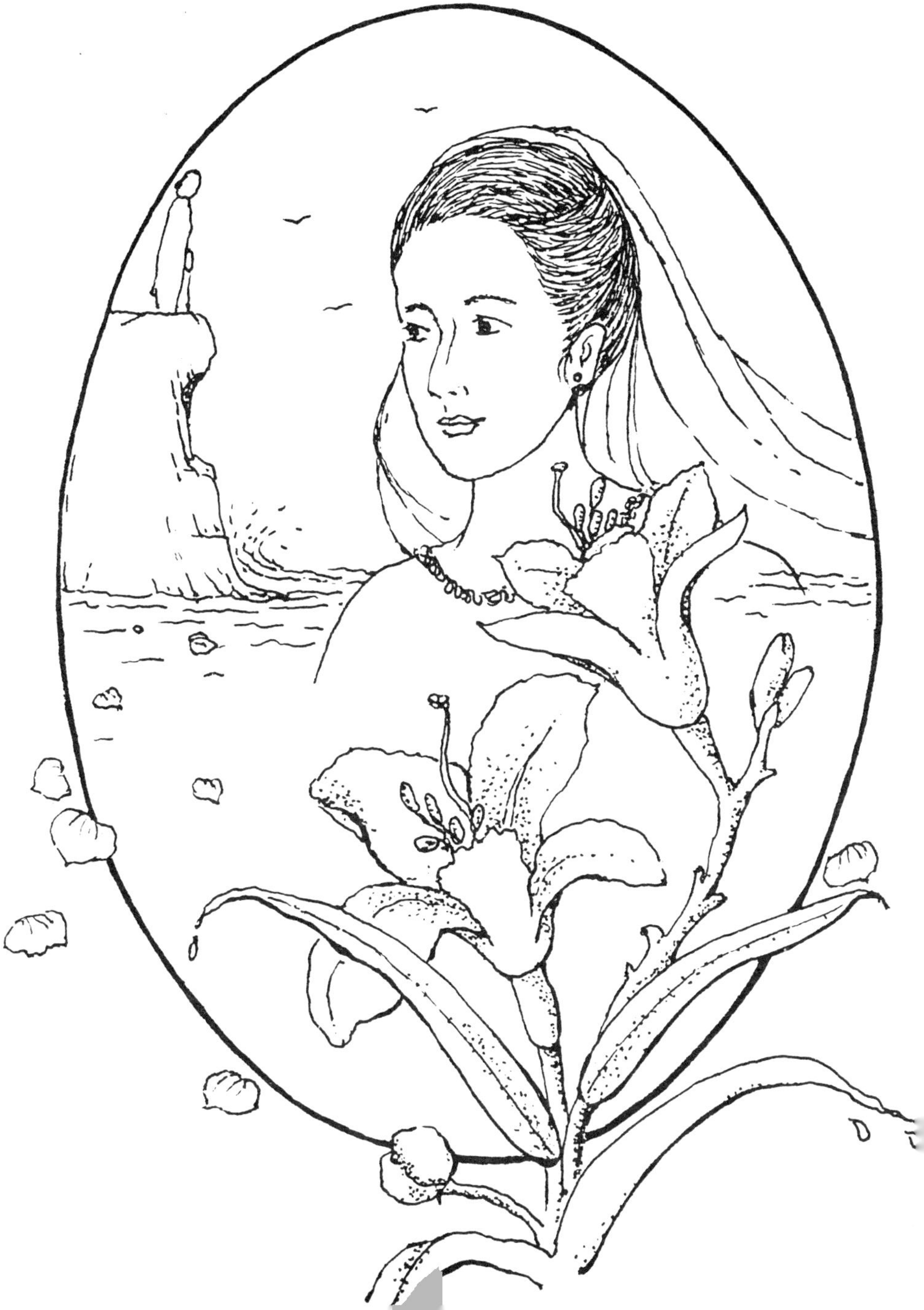

懷思

之一

也曾有過絢麗的夢
披一襲白紗曳地
捧一束紅花嬌艷
夢　乘著斑斕蝶翅
翅　飛向遙遠天際

也曾有過如幻憧憬
挽一隻堅壯臂膀
擁一簇親友祝福
幻　搭載於晶透蟬翼
翼　凋零於蕭殺秋後

挑一筐父母殷勤叮嚀

攜一篋少女天眞無畏

爲了泯不去的孝思

爲了止不住的仰慕

之二

擔一聲永遠的如夫人

扮一次無心的第三者

還是姻緣造成錯誤

是錯誤造成姻緣

之三

欲託終身只恨十幾寒暑

嘆相聚苦短

抑一臉愁容笑慰稚子

扛一肩家計身兼兩職

攝一幅溫馨圖　充思解念

捕一段刻骨情　療傷止悲

細數繾綣竟得四千朝夕

憶舊日情長

之四

是誰無心　提一句情為何物

是誰輕狂　捎一句生死相許

孤雁殉情　擇一處不離左右

英台化蝶　持一志日夜相伴

痴心空盼的望夫石

又豈怕相思來侵

最難　咬牙存活的人

捺一顆敏銳哀戚的心靈

拭一遍履遭啃噬的傷口／

最苦　失去港灣的船

搏一場暴風疾雨

擋一陣驚濤駭浪

之五

綜觀全局是必修課題

溫婉寬容是天生賦與

控一艘航艦　乘風破浪

揚一葉扁舟　悠游徜徉

金烏酡紅臉西墜

找不到落腳點　尋尋覓覓

撥一線瘖瘂琴弦

撩一簾薄暮春意

玉兔朦朧中東昇

照得屋裡屋外　冷冷清清

拒一彎新月如鈎

挨一夜蛙鼓蟲吟

淡月疏星　芳心悽悽

撚一燈如豆微光展讀

揉一團如雪片般來箋

曉星下沉　空閨慘慘

撒一地躁鬱煩悶

撿一襟寂寥落寞

晨曦初露　憂容戚戚

抹一頰烟脂　蒼白

掃一雙蛾眉　深鎖

之六

回首　黯然

揮一年又一年歲月

撕一頁又一頁日曆

觸目　悚然

拾一兜落髮　倏忽斑白

搔一頭青絲　曾經烏亮

也許　無情麻木了至情

也許　至情昇華了無情

擲一生青春年華　無悔

折一束修書

拈一撮馨香祝禱

摘一段詩詞吟誦

悼念維繫彼此

抒一己悼念

掬一眶熱淚懷思

抱一腔寸草感恩

之七

採一山青翠相伴

援一注水流廻盪

掩一坏黃土

黃土永隔天人

拋一切名利生命　無怨

修書寄託懷思

懷思恆久

恆久

懷

思

編後記

——創作是人生最榮耀的事業

陳韶華

　　『山動了』這本新詩集是我爲內子曾美霞女士所編輯出版的第四本書。

　　民國六十四年夏天，我和美霞在親友祝福聲中結婚；雖然我早知道內子喜愛文學，但卻遲至民國六十八年春天，她發表第一篇短篇小說時，我才驚喜的發現她的創作才能。因爲美霞擔任教職，空餘時間很有限．；於是，很自然的，我遂擔負起她的作品的編輯出版工作。

　　民國七十四年六月，內子的短篇小說結集出版；接著散文小品集問世；民國八十年七月，長篇小說『翩翩飛翔』連載後印行單行本。這本新詩集『山動了』就是她的第四本創作。

　　我從大學時代就開始寫作，我一直秉持——『創作是人生最榮耀的事業』的信念勇往直前，雖在十多年前我因故停筆，但我仍然

願以這則『創作是人生最榮耀的事業』的信念與内子曾美霞女士共勉之。

感謝綠蒂兄平時不吝對内子詩作的指導，尤其在百忙中更爲這本詩集寫序；還有陳春玉小姐爲這本詩集精心設計封面和繪製插圖，使這本詩集增加光采；在此特致十二萬分的謝意。但願不久，我有機會爲内子曾美霞女士的新作再盡一份編輯出版的心力，這是我所最期盼的事。

國家圖書館出版品預行編目資料

山動了 / 曾美霞著. -- 初版. -- 臺北市：文史
哲,民 92
　　面：　公分. -- (文史哲詩叢 ; 58)
　　ISBN 957-549-532-2 平裝)

851.86　　　　　　　　　　　　92020026

文史哲詩叢 ⑱

山　動　了

著　　者：曾　　　美　　　霞
　　　　　郵政劃撥 19659236 號陳逸多帳戶
出版者：文　史　哲　出　版　社
　　　　　http://www.lapen.com.tw
登記證字號：行政院新聞局版臺業字五三三七號
發行人：彭　　　正　　　雄
發行所：文　史　哲　出　版　社
印刷者：文　史　哲　出　版　社
　　　　　臺北市羅斯福路一段七十二巷四號
　　　　　郵政劃撥帳號：一六一八○一七五
　　　　　電話 886-2-23511028・傳真 886-2-23965656

實價新臺幣一六○元

中華民國八十一年 (1992) 八 月 初 版
中華民國九十二年 (2003) 十一月增訂初版

ISBN 957-549-532-2